This course will provide you with 20 easy ways to make money with artificial intelligence online. You can create a mobile app that uses AI to help people find the best deals on products or services, build an AI-based chatbot for customer service, design a virtual assistant to answer questions and suggest products, develop a search engine using AI algorithms, and create personalized content for websites or blogs. You can also sell digital products that use AI, offer an online course teaching people how to program AI-based systems, build a job search engine using AI, provide marketing services using AI data analysis, develop energy efficiency solutions with AI, use AI for content generation for websites or social media posts, create a software solution that automates mundane tasks using AI, create an app that uses AI to recommend restaurants and attractions, develop text analytics solutions with AI, build a chatbot using natural language processing algorithms, provide automated administrative tasks with AI-powered automation tools, create an AI-driven facial recognition system for security protocols, create a virtual assistant that understands user queries, offer AI-based customer service solutions, and develop a voice recognition system that can understand spoken commands.

With these 20 ways to make money online with artificial intelligence, you'll be able to capitalize on the latest technology for financial success.

Note: If you need help creating any of these computer programs or apps you can hire a freelancer for a small price on Fiverr.com. Just give them my course outline and they can do the rest. Good Luck.

TABLE OF CONTENTS

Chapter 1: Create a mobile app that uses artificial intelligence to help people find the best deals on products or services they are interested in.

Step 1: Research the market to determine what types of products or services people are looking for. How do you research the market? You can use online surveys, interviews, and focus groups to understand consumer needs and preferences.

Step 2: Identify the technologies needed for your app. This includes AI algorithms, language processing techniques, search engine optimization techniques and more. Where can you find the technologies needed for the app? Use sources like the Google Cloud Platform, Amazon's Alexa Skills Kit and Microsoft Azure to find technologies for your app.

Step 3: Develop the user interface of your app. The UI should be designed in a way that makes it easy for users to navigate and find what they are looking for. Consider using tools like Appcelerator or Xamarin to develop the UI. Develop a prototype for your mobile app.

This should include features such as natural language processing (NLP) so that users can type or speak their queries; using semantic

analysis to understand user intent; and incorporating machine learning models to personalize results according to user preference.

Step 4: Design an algorithm that will enable your AI-powered app to detect patterns in user behavior, identify trends in data, and suggest best deals on products or services based on user preferences. You can use machine learning algorithms such as linear regression, decision trees, random forests, and deep learning networks to create this algorithm.

Step 5: Test and tune your app to ensure it is delivering the best possible results. Test different algorithms, tweak the user interface, and measure the results of each iteration. Test the app with a small test group to ensure that it is functioning properly before releasing it to the public.

Step 6: Deploy your AI-powered app and make sure it is accessible to users on a range of devices. Use tools like App Store Optimization (ASO) or Google Play store optimization to help you get more downloads for your app. When you deploy the app monitor it for user feedback. Make changes as needed to improve its usability and performance.

Step 7: Promote the app to different target audiences to increase adoption. Utilize marketing strategies such as social media campaigns, influencer partnerships, or search engine optimization tactics.

Finally, use analytics to track user engagement and improve the performance of your app over time. Analyzing data will enable you to tweak settings, optimize features and refine algorithms to deliver the best possible experience for users. With these steps, you can create a mobile app that uses AI to help people find the best deals on products or services they are interested in! Good luck!

Chapter 2. Develop an AI-based chatbot to provide customer service and technical support for your website or business.

Step 1: Determine the type of customer service or technical support that your chatbot will provide. Will it be a general-purpose bot providing generic help or one that is tailored to certain types of questions? The more specific and focused the chatbot's purpose, the better the results it will deliver.

Step 2: Collect data and build a corpus of messages that you want the chatbot to understand.

This process can be automated by using existing public datasets or manually compiled through customer service logs.

Step 3: Choose an AI-based platform to develop your chatbot. Popular options include Amazon Lex, Google Dialogflow, Microsoft Bot Framework, and IBM Watson Conversation Service.

Step 4: Train the chatbot on sample conversations to teach it how to respond to various inquiries from customers. Make sure to use several different types of questions to give your bot a well-rounded understanding of its purpose.

Step 5: Test the chatbot's responses with actual users before launching it on your website or business. This is essential to ensuring the chatbot delivers an effective and accurate customer service experience.

Step 6: Monitor user feedback and data after launch, to identify and improve any weaknesses that may exist in your chatbot's performance. With continued optimization and testing, you can continually refine the bot's conversational abilities over time.

By following these steps, you can create an AI-based chatbot for customer service or technical support on your website or business. Good luck!

Chapter 3. Design an AI-powered virtual assistant that can answer questions, recommend products, and provide helpful information.

Step 1: Determine the purpose of your virtual assistant. Will it be a general-purpose assistant or one focused on specific tasks? Your choice will depend on the type of service you provide and its target audience. expand this step

Step 2: Design the user interface of your virtual assistant. Consider creating natural language processing (NLP) capabilities to make the experience more interactive and engaging for users. Gather data to train the virtual assistant. This can include publicly available datasets, customer logs, or any other source of relevant information that may help teach the assistant how to respond to inquiries.

Step 3: Implement AI algorithms such as machine learning, natural language processing (NLP), or computer vision to power your virtual assistant.

You can either use existing frameworks or develop custom models depending on your specific requirements.

Choose an AI-based platform for developing your virtual assistant. Popular options include Amazon Alexa, Google Assistant, Microsoft Cortana, and IBM Watson Assistant.

Step 4: Develop a knowledge graph that contains all relevant information about topics you want the virtual assistant to cover. This will enable it to provide accurate answers quickly. Train your virtual assistant using sample conversations and questions in order to teach it how to respond appropriately to different inquiries.

Step 5: Test the performance of your virtual assistant with actual users before releasing it into production. Make sure to measure key metrics such as accuracy, response time, and user satisfaction. Make sure to cover a wide range of scenarios to ensure the assistant can answer questions accurately and provide helpful information.

Step 6: Monitor user feedback and data after launch, in order to identify and improve any weaknesses that may exist in your assistant's performance.

With continued optimization and testing, you can continually refine your virtual assistant's conversational abilities over time.

By following these steps, you can create an AI-powered virtual assistant that can answer questions, recommend products, and provide helpful information! Good luck!

Chapter 4. Create a search engine that uses artificial intelligence to improve user experience and generate targeted ads.

Step 1: Create a database of information related to the topics or products your search engine will cover. This may include publicly available datasets, customer logs, or any other source of relevant information. Determine the features and capabilities you wish to include in your search engine. This could include natural language processing, semantic analysis, machine learning algorithms, and image recognition technology.

Step 2: Develop or use existing algorithms such as natural language processing (NLP) and machine learning in order to parse user queries and accurately match them with relevant results. Design a user-friendly interface for your search engine that encourages people to use it often. Create an intuitive navigation system with relevant categories and options that make it easy for users to find what they're looking for.

Step 3: Implement data-driven techniques such as collaborative filtering to provide personalized search results based on user behavior and past searches. This can help make the search experience more intuitive for users. Gather data in order to train the search engine AI algorithms. Sources of data may include web pages, text documents, images, videos, or any other relevant material. Be sure to review all collected data for accuracy as this will ensure correct results when searching.

Step 4: Integrate automated processes such as voice recognition into the search engine in order to make it easier for users to find what they are looking for quickly. Develop the search engine's AI algorithms and integrate them into the user interface. This could include natural language processing (NLP), machine learning (ML) models, or any other relevant technology.

Step 5: Utilize AI-driven recommendation systems to generate targeted ads based on user searches. This can help increase the effectiveness of your advertising campaigns by delivering more relevant content to users. Implement targeted advertising capabilities in your search engine. Create an algorithm that identifies content related to users' searches, so you can generate targeted ads for products and services they may be interested in.

Step 6: Monitor user feedback and data after launch, in order to identify and improve any weaknesses that may exist in your search engine's performance. With continued optimization and testing, you can continually refine your search engine's capabilities over time. Test your search engine with a small group of users before launching it publicly. Monitor key metrics such as accuracy, response time, and user satisfaction to identify any issues and make improvements where necessary.

By following these steps, you can create an AI-powered search engine that can accurately process queries and deliver personalized results! Good luck!

Chapter 5. Use AI-based algorithms to create personalized content for your website or blog.

Step 1: Identify the purpose of the chatbot and what tasks it should be able to perform for users. This could include answering frequently asked questions. Collect data about user preferences and behavior. This can include website logs, customer reviews, and any other relevant source of information. You will use this information to create personalized content for each user.

Step 2: Develop algorithms that can identify patterns in the collected data. For example, you could use machine learning (ML) or natural language processing (NLP) algorithms to analyze text or image data. The aim is to generate insights into users' desires and interests based on their past behaviors.

Step 3: Use AI-driven recommendation systems to provide tailored content suggestions for each individual user. This could be in the form of product recommendations, content curation, or targeted ads based on an analysis of a user's past behavior.

Step 4: Monitor the success of your personalized content campaigns and adjust accordingly. Analyze metrics such as click-through rate (CTR), engagement time, and satisfaction ratings to determine if your efforts have been effective or not. Make necessary changes based on these results in order to maximize the impact of your personalized content campaigns.

By using AI-based algorithms for personalization, you can create tailored content that resonates with each individual user, leading to higher engagement rates and improved customer satisfaction! Good luck!

Chapter 6. Sell digital products, such as templates or tools, which use Artificial Intelligence in their functionality.

Step 1: Identify the digital products you would like to offer. These could include templates, tools, apps, and other software that utilizes AI algorithms for its functionality.

Step 2: Develop your product's AI capabilities. This includes training and refining relevant machine learning (ML) models or natural language processing (NLP) algorithms. Make sure your product works reliably and efficiently.

Step 3: Create a website or landing page where customers can learn more about your product and purchase it. Provide detailed information on how the product works and what features it has. Highlight any unique benefits of using an AI-driven solution over traditional alternatives.

Step 4: Promote your digital product online via social media platforms, blogs, Google Ads, etc. Encourage users to try your product for free before committing to a purchase.

Step 5: Use analytics tools to monitor the performance of your digital products. Track key metrics such as customer acquisition rate, churn rate, and usage frequency in order to identify any potential optimization opportunities or areas needing improvement.

By following these steps and leveraging AI-based solutions in your digital products, you can create valuable offerings that stand out from the competition! Good luck!

Chapter 7. Develop and offer an online course to teach people how to use and program AI-based systems.

Step 1: Identify the topics you would like to teach in your course. This could include topics such as machine learning (ML), natural language processing (NLP), computer vision, or other AI-related concepts.

Step 2: Develop a comprehensive curriculum for your course. Curate content that covers the basics of AI programming and build up from there to more complex algorithms and applications. Mention any real-world use cases and provide practical examples whenever possible.

Step 3: Create instructional videos and other materials to supplement the course content. Use visuals and animation wherever necessary to make your lessons easier to comprehend.

Step 4: Set up an online platform where students can access their course materials, participate in discussions, and receive feedback from the instructor.

Step 5: Promote your course to potential customers via digital marketing channels such as social media and Google Ads. Offer discounts and free trials to encourage more people to sign up for your course.

By following these steps, you can create an engaging online course that teaches students how to use AI-based systems! Good luck!

Chapter 8. Create an AI-powered job search engine that can find the best opportunities for job seekers.

Step 1: Research the existing job search engines and identify the features that would make your AI-powered version stand out from the competition.

Step 2: Design a database to store information about job postings, such as company details, salary range, required skills, etc. This data can be used to index jobs for better search results.

Step 3: Develop an AI algorithm that can learn from users' searches and suggest relevant job openings based on their preferences and experience.

Step 4: Create a user-friendly interface for your job search engine where people can quickly find jobs according to their criteria. Allow them to save favorite jobs or create custom alerts when new opportunities arise.

Step 5: Promote your job search engine on social media, blogs and other digital marketing channels. Invite people to try it out and provide feedback to help you continue optimizing the product.

By taking these steps, you can create an AI-powered job search engine that helps people find the best opportunities for them and make their job hunting experience easier! Good luck!

Chapter 9. Offer marketing services to businesses, utilizing Artificial Intelligence for data analysis, customer segmentation, lead generation, and more.

Step 1: Identify the AI-based solutions that can be used to improve marketing processes, such as customer segmentation, lead generation, and predictive analytics.

Step 2: Research existing technologies and products that are available on the market to identify the most suitable options for your clients' needs.

Step 3: Gather relevant data from sources including social media platforms, web traffic analytics, CRM systems, and other databases. Utilize AI algorithms to analyze this data and generate insights about customer behavior.

Step 4: Develop a personalized marketing strategy for each of your clients based on the insights generated by AI-driven analysis. This could include targeted ads and messaging across multiple channels such as email newsletters or social media.

Step 5: Track and measure the outcomes of your AI-based marketing campaigns to adjust them as needed. Utilize performance metrics such as click-through rate, conversion rate, or customer lifetime value to assess their success.

By following these steps, you can offer marketing services that utilize Artificial Intelligence to help businesses better understand their customers and reach out to them with personalized offers! Good luck!

Chapter 10. Offer AI-driven energy efficiency solutions to households and businesses.

Step 1: Research existing AI-driven energy efficiency solutions and identify the features that would make your offering stand out from the competition.

Step 2: Design an AI algorithm that can analyze data from connected devices such as smart thermostats, smart lights, power meters, etc. to identify opportunities for energy savings.

Step 3: Develop user-friendly interfaces and reports to inform customers about their current energy usage patterns and potential areas of improvement.

Step 4: Integrate with existing systems like HVAC control panels or lighting systems to enable automated optimization of energy consumption based on customer preferences.

Step 5: Promote your solution via digital marketing channels such as social media and Google Ads. Invite customers to try it out and provide feedback to further optimize the product.

By taking these steps, you can create an AI-driven energy efficiency solution that helps households and businesses save money and reduce their carbon footprint! Good luck!

Chapter 11. Use Artificial Intelligence algorithms to create content for websites or social media posts.

Step 1: Research existing AI-based content creation tools and identify the features that would be suitable for your needs.

Step 2: Build an algorithm to generate relevant topics based on user input or content from external sources.

Step 3: Integrate natural language processing (NLP) techniques to create text that reads like it was written by a human.

Step 4: Optimize the generated text with AI algorithms such as deep learning and reinforcement learning to refine the results further.

Step 5: Test your solution on sample websites or social media posts and collect feedback from users about its accuracy and relevance.

By taking these steps, you can use Artificial Intelligence algorithms to create unique and engaging content for websites or social media posts that will help you reach your audience efficiently. Good luck!

Chapter 12. Develop a software solution that uses AI to automate mundane tasks such as data entry, financial analysis, or customer service.

Step 1: Research existing AI-based automation tools and identify the features that would be suitable for your needs.

Step 2: Design an AI algorithm to automate basic tasks such as data entry or financial analysis. This could involve utilizing techniques such as natural language processing, machine learning, and neural networks.

Step 3: Integrate the AI solution with existing software and databases to maximize efficiency.

Step 4: Perform testing and optimization of the algorithm to ensure accuracy and scalability.

Step 5: Develop a user-friendly interface that makes it easy for customers to access automated services.

Step 6: Leverage data analytics to identify trends and insights from the automated processes. This can help you further optimize your AI solution and uncover new opportunities for improvement.

Step 7: Develop a customer service automation AI system that is capable of responding to basic inquiries with personalized answers quickly and accurately. This can improve customer satisfaction by providing a more efficient customer service experience.

Step 8: Utilize AI-based analytics and machine learning to monitor the performance of automated tasks. This can help you identify areas where improvements are needed, so you can ensure that your solution is constantly optimized.

By taking these steps, you will be able to develop an AI-driven automation software solution that can help businesses reduce costs and improve efficiency. Good luck!

Chapter 13. Create an app that uses AI to recommend restaurants or attractions based on user preferences.

Step 1: Research existing AI-based recommendation tools and identify the features that would be suitable for your needs. When researching existing AI-based recommendation tools, look at features like natural language processing, machine learning algorithms that can analyze user preferences data, integration with online databases or platforms, data mining techniques to collect reviews and ratings related to restaurants or attractions, algorithms to prioritize recommendations based on user preferences, and a user-friendly interface that makes it easy for customers to access recommended restaurants or attractions.

Step 2: Design an algorithm to collect user preferences data, such as preferred cuisine or price range. This could involve utilizing techniques such as natural language processing, machine learning, and neural networks.

When designing an algorithm to collect user preferences data, consider utilizing techniques such as natural language processing (NLP) to understand customer questions and requests and machine learning algorithms that can analyze gathered user preferences data.

Additionally, you could also use neural network-based algorithms to identify patterns or trends in user data.

Step 3: Integrate the AI solution with existing databases or online platforms to access relevant information about restaurants and attractions. Integrating the AI-based recommendation system with existing databases or online platforms can allow you to quickly and easily access relevant information about restaurants or attractions to generate recommendations for users. This could involve using web APIs from providers such as Google Place or Yelp.

Step 4: Use data mining techniques to collect user ratings, reviews, and other data related to restaurants or attractions. This can help you create an accurate recommendation system for users. Data mining techniques can be used to gather user ratings, reviews, and other data related to restaurants or attractions. This data can then be used to create an accurate recommendation system that is tailored to each user's preferences. Examples of data mining techniques include text analysis, sentiment analysis, predictive analytics, and clustering algorithms.

Step 5: Create an algorithm that prioritizes recommendations based on user preferences. This could involve using techniques such as collaborative filtering and content-based filtering. When creating an algorithm to prioritize recommendations, consider using techniques such as collaborative filtering and content-based filtering. Collaborative filtering algorithms use input from other users with similar tastes or preferences to recommend items. Content-based filtering algorithms look at the description of each item and recommend items that match certain keywords or criteria.

Step 6: Design a user-friendly interface that makes it easy for customers to access recommended restaurants or attractions. This could involve features such as maps, filters, and search tools. When designing the user interface for the app, consider incorporating features such as interactive maps that show the locations of recommended restaurants or attractions, customizable filters that let customers narrow down the recommendations to their particular preferences, and powerful search tools that allow users to quickly find what they are looking for. Additionally, make sure the interface is easy to navigate and understand.

With these steps in place, you can create an AI-based recommendation system that offers customers personalized recommendations tailored to their individual needs. This can help businesses better engage their customers and increase customer satisfaction.

Chapter 14. Develop an AI-driven text analytics solution for businesses that can extract insights from unstructured data.

Step 1: Collect unstructured data from various sources such as customer reviews and feedback, social media posts, surveys, blogs, etc. This can be done by using web scrapers to collect the data or leveraging APIs from major social media platforms such as Facebook and Twitter.

Step 2: Utilize natural language processing (NLP) techniques such as sentiment analysis and topic modeling to extract insights from the data. Sentiment analysis involves using algorithms to detect whether a particular text is positive, negative, or neutral in tone while topic modeling involves identifying topics that are present in the data.

Step 3: Create an algorithm that can accurately classify the text into predefined categories. This could involve using supervised learning techniques such as decision tree algorithms, support vector machines (SVMs), or artificial neural networks. These algorithms can be trained to identify and classify the text into the appropriate categories.

Step 4: Analyze the results to identify patterns and trends in the data that can be used to gain insights. This could involve extracting keywords or topics of particular interest and using them to gain insights into customer preferences, market trends, etc.

Step 5: Deploy the text analytics solution in a production environment, allowing businesses to use the insights gained from the text analytics solution to make more informed decisions. This could involve integrating the solution with existing business systems such as customer relationship management (CRM) systems, marketing automation tools, or enterprise resource planning (ERP) solutions.

By following these steps and utilizing AI-driven text analytics solutions, businesses can gain valuable insights from unstructured data and use those insights to drive their decision-making process. This can help them better understand their customers and markets, resulting in improved customer satisfaction and increased profits.

Chapter 15. Create a chatbot that uses natural language processing algorithms to respond to customer inquiries quickly and accurately.

Step 1: Designing a conversational user interface involves creating different types of questions and responses that the chatbot will use to interact with customers. This could include common customer inquiries such as "What are your store hours?" or "Do you have any sales right now?" In addition, it is important to create an engaging dialogue format by utilizing natural language processing techniques such as sentiment analysis and entity recognition. This helps make conversations more human-like and allows customers to feel comfortable interacting with the chatbot.

Step 2: Utilize natural language processing algorithms to process incoming queries from customers. This can involve creating rules-based algorithms or using supervised learning models like decision trees, support vector machines (SVMs), or neural networks to detect the type of query that a customer is asking and how it should be responded to. Additionally, this step can involve leveraging existing datasets such as OpenAI's GPT-3 model or IBM Watson's natural language processing library to provide more accurate results.

Step 3: Once the type of query has been identified, implement an appropriate response. This could involve providing a direct answer to the customer's question, redirecting them to another resource or page within the website, or offering helpful advice based on their query. The chatbot should also be programmed with error-handling capabilities so that if it does not understand a query it can ask for clarification from the customer or provide a list of possible solutions for them to choose from.

Step 4: Finally, test and deploy the chatbot in a production environment. This could involve using existing customer service systems such as live chat software or creating a standalone chatbot that can be integrated into existing business platforms. Additionally, it is important to regularly monitor and update the algorithm to ensure accuracy and functionality as customer inquiries evolve over time.

By utilizing natural language processing algorithms, businesses can create powerful chatbots that can process incoming queries quickly and accurately while providing an engaging experience for customers. With this technology, businesses can free up resources for more strategic tasks rather than responding to mundane customer queries which can help improve overall customer satisfaction.

Chapter 16. Use AI-powered automation tools to complete administrative tasks such as scheduling meetings, managing calendars, and more.

Step 1: Research and select the right automation tool. There are many AI-powered tools available on the market today with different features. To choose the best one for your business needs, make sure to consider factors such as price point, user reviews, integration capabilities, scalability, security protocols, customer service options, and project management capabilities. It is also important to take into account the size of your organization and its specific needs in order to ensure the automation tool meets all your requirements.

Step 2: Define what tasks you want the automation tool to manage. This could include scheduling meetings, inputting data into a system, organizing calendars, sending out automated reminders and notifications, generating reports, or tracking customer interactions. Once you have identified and documented these tasks, make sure the automation tool can support them and that they are set up correctly in its user interface.

Step 3: Train the AI-powered tools with real-world examples. This process involves inputting data and examples so the tool can learn how to complete tasks effectively. It's important to ensure that the tool is well-trained before deploying it in a production environment as this will help reduce errors and improve overall accuracy. This can be done through a process known as supervised learning where data sets are used to "train" the AI system, allowing it to recognize patterns and make predictions with greater accuracy.

Step 4: Deploy the automation tool in a production environment.

Once deployed, regularly monitor and test the tool to ensure it is working correctly and that it is meeting your business needs. Additionally, make sure the tool is consistently updated with new data so its accuracy remains high. This can be done through a process known as reinforcement learning where feedback from real-world usage is used to adjust the AI system's parameters. This can help keep the tool up-to-date with current conditions and make it more accurate in its predictions.

By utilizing AI-powered automation tools, businesses can automate mundane administrative tasks such as scheduling meetings, managing calendars, and generating reports. This can help free up resources and improve overall productivity while also increasing customer satisfaction. Additionally, businesses can save money on labor costs as they will no longer need to hire additional employees to manage these tasks. Furthermore, AI-powered automation can speed up processes by providing more accurate and timely responses for customers. Therefore, AI-powered automation can be a great way for businesses to streamline their operations and improve their bottom line.

Chapter 17. Develop an AI-driven facial recognition system to help businesses with security protocols.

Step 1: Research and select the right facial recognition technology. There are various AI-powered facial recognition technologies available on the market today so it's important to select one that meets your specific needs and budget. Make sure to consider factors such as accuracy, scalability, user access control, data security protocols, integration with existing systems, and customer service options when selecting the right technology for your business.

Step 2: Collect and organize the data necessary to power your facial recognition system. This can include user photos and other identifying information, such as name, age, gender etc. Be sure to store this data securely in order to protect it and comply with relevant privacy regulations.

Step 3: Train the facial recognition system. This involves providing it with data sets and examples so it can learn how to accurately recognize faces. It's important to use high-quality images for training in order to get the most accurate results. Additionally, make sure that you are handling your data safely and responsibly by keeping user information secure and respecting privacy regulations.

Step 4: Deploy and monitor the system in your production environment. This process involves setting up the facial recognition system and making sure it is running correctly with all of the necessary features enabled.

Additionally, make sure to regularly test and monitor the system to ensure it is meeting your needs, as well as any relevant security protocols.

Step 5: Establish protocols for handling false positives. False positives can occur when a system misidentifies a person, which can lead to serious consequences in certain situations. To prevent this, businesses must establish clear protocols that allow users to quickly and easily report errors or discrepancies in the facial recognition system. Additionally, make sure to analyze any reported false positives in order to identify and address any potential issues with the algorithm or data sets.

Step 6: Consider implementing additional security measures. While facial recognition can be a powerful tool for protecting your business, it should not be used as the only security measure. To ensure maximum protection, consider integrating other forms of biometric authentication such as fingerprint scanning, voice recognition, or iris scanning. Additionally, consider implementing additional security protocols such as two-factor authentication or advanced encryption to further safeguard sensitive information.

By following these steps and taking the necessary precautions, businesses can make sure that their facial recognition system is secure and reliable. With a well-implemented AI-driven facial recognition system, businesses can enjoy increased security and improved customer service.

As the technology continues to evolve, organizations should stay up-to-date on the latest best practices in order to ensure maximum protection for their customers and employees.

Additionally, consider implementing regular training programs for employees who will be using or interacting with facial recognition systems. By familiarizing themselves with the technology, employees can better understand how it works and help ensure that customers' data is being handled properly. With the right precautions in place, businesses can feel confident when implementing facial recognition technology.

This is an exciting time for businesses who are looking to implement AI-driven Facial Recognition systems into their operations. By following the steps outlined above, businesses can ensure that their facial recognition system is secure and reliable – while also providing added convenience and security to customers. With the right precautions in place, businesses will be able to fully benefit from all of the advantages that facial recognition systems have to offer.

Chapter 18. Create a virtual assistant that can understand user queries and provide accurate answers or recommendations.

Step 1: Select an appropriate platform for building your virtual assistant. There are many different platforms available, including but not limited to Amazon Alexa, Google Assistant, Microsoft Cortana, and Apple Siri. Each platform has its own advantages and disadvantages, so it's important to select the one that best fits your needs.

Step 2: Establish the scope and purpose of your virtual assistant. Think about who will be using the virtual assistant, what types of questions it should be able to answer (e.g., customer service inquiries, product recommendations), and any additional capabilities you may want it to have (e.g., access to third-party services).

Step 3: Design and build the conversational interface. This includes creating a dialogue that will allow users to interact with your virtual assistant, such as providing responses to inquiries or displaying recommended products. Make sure that it is easy for users to understand and use.

Step 4: Develop natural language processing (NLP) capabilities. NLP allows your virtual assistant to better interpret user queries and provide accurate answers. This may involve training the virtual assistant on a dataset that includes conversations or commands as well as developing algorithms to automate responses.

Step 5: Test your virtual assistant before releasing it publicly. During this stage, you should test for accuracy, clarity of dialogue, ease of use, and security features. This is also the time to add any additional features or capabilities you may want your virtual assistant to have.

Step 6: Release your virtual assistant and monitor its performance. Once it's released, you should continue to test and evaluate its performance in order to further optimize the experience for users. This may include adding new features, changing the dialogue, or collecting user feedback.

By following these steps, you can create a virtual assistant that can understand user queries and provide accurate answers or recommendations. With proper design and implementation, businesses can take advantage of this technology to improve customer service, increase productivity, and reduce costs. By staying up to date on the latest best practices in designing conversational interfaces and developing NLP capabilities, businesses can ensure that their virtual assistant is easy to use and delivers the best results.

Chapter 19. Offer AI-based solutions for customer service, such as automated customer support, live chatbots, and more.

Step 1: Choose the right platform for your AI-based customer service solutions. Popular platforms include Amazon Alexa, Google Assistant, and Chatfuel. Before deciding which one is best for you, consider what features and capabilities are offered by each platform. For example, some platforms offer pre-built tools or services that can help you to quickly create automated customer support or live chatbots. Others may provide more customization options but require more development time and effort on your part.

Step 2: Develop an automated customer support system. This system can be used to provide customers with answers to common questions or direct them to the correct resources based on their query. You can create a text-based or voice-based automated customer support system depending on the needs of your business. For example, if you are providing customer service in a retail setting, a voice-based system might be more effective as customers can easily ask questions and get answers without having to type anything.

Step 3: Create a live chatbot that can interact with customers in real time. Live chatbots use natural language processing (NLP) to understand user queries and provide accurate answers or direct them to the right resources. When designing your chatbot, think about how you want it to interact with customers and what information you want it to have access to in order to give meaningful responses.

Additionally, make sure that your chatbot is able to store customer data securely and comply with any applicable privacy regulations.

Step 4: Establish metrics for measuring success. This will allow you to track how well your AI-based customer service solutions are performing so that you can make any necessary changes or improvements. Common performance metrics include response times, accuracy of answers, customer satisfaction ratings, and engagement rates. Additionally, it's important to measure which features customers are using most so that you can optimize the user experience and ensure that your solutions meet their needs.

By following these steps, businesses can take advantage of AI-based customer service solutions to provide customers with an improved experience. Automated support systems can increase efficiency by reducing wait times and freeing up staff to focus on more complex issues. Live chatbots can provide customers with 24/7 support without the need for a human agent and can even help to generate leads. With the right strategy, AI-based customer service solutions can become an invaluable asset for businesses looking to improve their customer experience. Good luck!

Chapter 20. Develop a voice recognition system that can understand spoken commands and respond accordingly.

Step 1: Select a platform for your voice recognition system. Popular platforms include Amazon Alexa, Google Assistant, and Cortana. Before selecting one, consider the features and capabilities of each platform. For example, look at their natural language processing (NLP) capabilities to make sure it can accurately interpret user requests as well as their integration with other software such as customer relationship management (CRM) or enterprise resource planning (ERP) systems. Additionally, check to see if they provide any customization options that allow you to tailor the system to your needs such as custom intents or entities.

Step 2: Develop conversational user interfaces (CUIs) that can understand spoken commands from users and respond accordingly. To do this, you will need to create intents, entities, and dialogs for your system to use when recognizing user requests. Intents define what action the user wants to take (e.g., "get directions"), entities define the data associated with an intent (e.g., "restaurant name" in the case of the "get directions" intent), and dialogs define the logic for how your system will respond to a user request (e.g., how it will confirm that it has received and understood the command). You can also create custom intents or entities specific to your business that are not available through out-of-the-box options on your chosen platform.

Step 3: Write code to integrate your CUIs with your chosen platform. This may involve writing a custom skill or integrating an existing one into your platform. For example, if you are using Amazon Alexa, you can write code in Node.js to create a custom skill that responds to spoken commands from users. Additionally, you can use APIs and libraries provided by the platform to access data stored on their servers as well as send messages back to the user such as confirmation messages or error notifications.

Step 4: Test and debug your voice recognition system. To do this, you should have some test users try out the system and provide feedback on their experience. Additionally, use analytics tools such as Google Analytics or Amazon Insights to track how well the system is performing and identify any areas that need improvement. Finally, employ techniques such as A/B testing to ensure that the system is responding correctly to user requests and providing the best possible experience.

By following these steps, you can develop a voice recognition system that can understand spoken commands and respond accordingly. With the right strategy and implementation, you can create an effective voice recognition system that meets your customers' needs and provides them with an improved experience. Good luck!

Note: If you need help creating any of these computer programs or apps you can hire a freelancer for a small price on Fiverr.com. Just give them my course online and they can do the rest. Good Luck.